FAVORITE TOYS

MADE FROM

FAILURES

FANTASTIC FAILURES

From Flops to Fortune

MARTIN GITLIN

45 45TH PARALLEL PRESS

Published in the United States of America by Cherry Lake Publishing Group
Ann Arbor, Michigan
www.cherrylakepublishing.com

Reading Adviser: Beth Walker Gambro, MS, Ed., Reading Consultant, Yorkville, IL
Series Adviser: Virginia Loh-Hagan
Book Designer: Frame25 Productions

Photo Credits: © Kostenko Iryna/Shutterstock, cover, title page; © Warut Chinsai/Shutterstock, 4; © Mila Supinskaya Glashchenko/Shutterstock, 5; © Chaosamran_Studio/Shutterstock, 7; Public domain, United States Patent Office, 8; Unknown author, Public domain, via Wikimedia Commons, 9; ell brown, CC BY-SA 2.0 via Wikimedia Commons, 10; © shapovalphoto/Shutterstock, 11; © The Image Party/Shutterstock, 12; Toledo-Lucas County Public Library, Public domain, via Wikimedia Commons, 15; JacobZufall, CC BY-SA 4.0 via Wikimedia Commons, 16; © Ilina Yuliia/Shutterstock, 17; © Ilina Yuliia/Shutterstock, 18; © Ekaterina79/Dreamstime.com, 19; Foto: Stefan Brending, Public domain via Wikimedia Commons, 20; © l i g h t p o e t/Shutterstock, 23; © Audio und werbung/Shutterstock, 24; U.S. National Archives and Records Administration, Public domain, via Wikimedia Commons, 25; © AS photo family/Shutterstock, 26; © charnsitr/Shutterstock, 27; Kansas City Chiefs, Public domain, via Wikimedia Commons, 28; Lenore Edman, CC BY 2.0 via Wikimedia Commons, 29; © Alena A/Shutterstock, 32

45th Parallel Press is an imprint of Cherry Lake Publishing Group.

Library of Congress Cataloging-in-Publication Data has been filed and is available at catalog.loc.gov

Cherry Lake Publishing would like to acknowledge the work of the Partnership for 21st Century Learning, a network of Battelle for Kids. Please visit Battelle for Kids online for more information.

Printed in the United States of America

Note from publisher: Websites change regularly, and their future contents are outside of our control. Supervise children when conducting any recommended online searches for extended learning opportunities.

Contents

INTRODUCTION

"If at first you don't succeed, try, try again." This is an old saying. It's been said a lot. It's a great tip. Failure is part of life. It's not bad. It can have good results. People must not let failure defeat them. They should keep trying. Failing can lead to success.

Toy inventors learn from their mistakes. They know about failing. They have ideas. But not all ideas work. Some ideas **flop**. *Flop* means to fail. Ideas may not work as planned. Successful people don't give up.

They solve problems. They find other uses for flops. They turn flops into fortunes.

The toy business world has many examples. Many great products started as failures. These failures worked out. They didn't start as toys. But they ended up being a hit. They made life more fun.

Successful toy inventors show **persistence**. Persisting means not quitting. Their hard work paid off. That is a lesson everyone can learn.

CHAPTER 1

The Slinky: A Failed Spring That Walks

The year was 1943. Millions of American soldiers were overseas. They were fighting in World War II (1939–1945). Other soldiers stayed in the United States. They still helped the war effort. Among them was Richard James. James was a U.S. Navy **engineer**. Engineers build and design things.

James was trying to make springs. Springs were needed on ships. They helped to steady gear. But things weren't working for James. He kept failing.

Spring samples were on a shelf. One day, James knocked a few samples off the shelf. This was an accident. Then something odd happened. The springs fell. They hit the ground. But they didn't sit still. The metal wires "walked." They walked across the floor. They moved gracefully. James watched. He took it home. He showed his wife, Betty. James and Betty were amazed.

James wasn't mad. He wasn't defeated. He kept inventing. He thought of another use for the springs. He thought they'd make a fun toy. Betty thought so too. They worked together.

First, they needed a name. They studied the dictionary. They looked for an ideal word. Betty liked "Slinky." She thought it described the toy's walking motion.

James wasted no time. He was a great engineer. He designed a machine to make the new toy. His machine coiled 80 feet (24.4 meters) of wire into a 2.5-inch (6.35 centimeters) spiral.

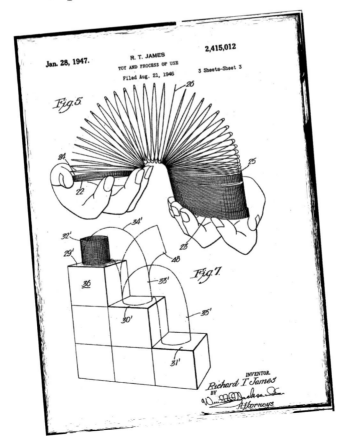

The couple needed money. They borrowed $500. They **manufactured** the new toy. Manufacture means to make in large numbers. The Slinky was born.

The couple created their own company. It was called James Industries. They waited until the holiday season in 1945. The war was now over. The couple knew people bought toys for Christmas. They went to Philadelphia, Pennsylvania. James and Betty showed off their toy at Gimbels. Gimbels was a popular department store. Many people shopped there.

The outcome was amazing. The store stocked 400 Slinkys that day. They sold out. This happened in less than 2 hours. Everyone wanted a Slinky. The Slinky was a must-have toy.

Slinky sales soared. Kids placed the Slinky on top of the stairs. They let it go. They watched it walk down the stairs.

The Slinky didn't always work. Some buyers complained. Some stairs were too tall. The toy failed to walk down each step. James kept working on it. Sales kept growing.

The Slinky had a famous **jingle**. Jingles are catchy slogans. They're used to sell products. The Slinky jingle is: "A spring, a spring, a marvelous thing! Everyone knows it's Slinky!" This jingle increased sales.

Everyone loves the Slinky. Philadelphia even hosts a National Slinky Day. This happens every August 30. By 2019, more than 360 million Slinkys had been sold!

Today, there are many Slinky toys. Some look like animals. An example is the Slinky Dog. Some look like people. Examples are Slinky Suzie and Slinky Crazy Eyes.

There are other uses for the wire toy. American soldiers used them as radio antennas. The Slinky even went into space. An astronaut showed how it behaved in zero gravity. It didn't walk. It just drooped.

James quit the company in 1960. Betty took over. She insisted on keeping the toy cheap. She wanted all children to have one. She said, "So many children can't have expensive toys." She felt a duty to young children. Slinky toys are simply marvelous!

FLOPPED!
Cabbage Patch Snacktime Kids

The Cabbage Patch Kids are dolls. They were invented in 1983. They were a huge success. These dolls were made by Mattel. Mattel is a famous toy company. These dolls sold very well. They inspired spinoffs. Spinoffs are created from another product. An example was Cabbage Patch cereal. Another example was Cabbage Patch Snacktime Kids. This toy was released in 1986. It came with plastic fake food. Kids could feed the dolls. These dolls had two metal rollers for lips. Kids' hair and fingers were getting caught. Angry parents complained. Mattel offered a $40 refund. Parents still weren't happy. Mattel added warning stickers to the dolls. The Cabbage Patch Snacktime Kids were doomed. They were pulled off the market in 1997.

CHAPTER 2

Play-Doh®: Wallpaper Cleaner Turned Toy

· ·

Millions of kids love playing with Play-Doh®. But few know who to thank. Joe McVicker and Kay Zufall invented it. They're related by marriage.

It all started with their uncles. Their uncles were Cleo and Noah McVicker. Cleo McVicker worked for Kutol. Kutol was a failing soap company. Cleo McVicker invented a wallpaper cleaner in the late 1920s. The cleaner removed dirt left on walls. The dirt was from coal-burning stoves. This cleaner was a **putty**. Putty feels like dough.

Cleo McVicker had an idea. He and Noah McVicker sold the cleaner to Kroger. Kroger is a grocery store chain. This plan worked. The cleaner made money.

But there was a problem. The cleaner fell out of demand. This happened in the 1940s. Most people stopped using coal. They used natural gas instead. Gas stoves don't need coal. They didn't dirty the walls.

Kay Zufall (1927-2014)

Then **vinyl** wallpaper was invented. Vinyl is a strong plastic. Vinyl wallpaper could be cleaned easily. It just needs soap and water. This made the cleaner unnecessary.

This is when Joe McVicker and Kay Zufall came to the rescue. Zufall was a schoolteacher. She gave the putty to her students. The putty was squishy. Her students played with it. They had fun. They formed it into shapes.

McVicker also watched them. He saw the kids mold the putty into Christmas ornaments. That gave him an idea. McVicker had Kutol rebrand the product as a toy. The company added food coloring. They added a nice smell. This made the putty more appealing. It became more like modeling clay.

The toy took off. They thought about naming it Rainbow Modeling **Compound**. Compound means something made of 2 or more substances. This name wasn't cool. It didn't attract buyers. So Zufall and her husband named it Play-Doh®.

Kutol also changed its name. It became Rainbow Crafts. This happened in 1956. It sold white Play-Doh® in one-gallon cans. The toy was later packaged in smaller containers. It was soon made into different colors. There was red. There was blue. There was yellow. Today, there are more colors.

One problem was that the dough dried too quickly. So McVicker hired a **chemist**. Chemists study substances. McVicker created a new formula. This kept Play-Doh® **pliable**. Pliable means flexible. The toy could be played with for a long time.

McVicker sold Play-Doh® to schools. Big department stores sold it as well. The toy was featured on popular children's TV shows. Sales soared. Play-Doh® became global. It reached England, France, and Italy by 1964. By the year 2020, it had sold more than 3 billion cans. It's been sold in more than 80 countries.

Play-Doh® is more than just a toy. It's sticky. It has other uses. People use it to pick up broken glass bits. They use it as a cleaner. They push it between car seats. This picks up fallen food crumbs.

This toy is still popular. It's part of the National Hall of Fame. This happened in 1998. There's also a National Play-Doh® Day. This day is celebrated every September 16.

FLOPPED!
The Fall of Sky Dancer

Sky Dancer seemed like a simple toy. It was a doll. It had helicopter wings. A child pulled a string. This made the wings spin. The doll would fly into the air. This toy was made by the Galoob Toy Company. It was released in 1994. It was made in time for the holidays. The idea didn't flop. Kids liked the toy. Sky Dancer flopped because it was dangerous. It flew into people. It smacked kids. It damaged teeth. It damaged eyes. It even broke a rib. There were more than 170 reported injuries. It was taken off the market in 2000.

CHAPTER 3

The Super Ball® : From Rubber Goo to Super Toy

··

Norman Stingley created a big hit. This happened in 1964. His toy was called the Super Ball®. A year later, 6 million had been sold.

Stingley was a chemist. He worked for the Bettis Rubber Company. This company was in California. Stingley was playing with **synthetic** rubber. Synthetic means human-made.

The rubber was like goo. Stingley formed this goo into a ball. He used heavy pressure. He compressed it. He was surprised by the effect. The ball had an amazing bounce.

Stingley showed it to his company. But the Bettis Rubber Company wasn't interested. The Super Ball® wasn't super yet.

Stingley refused to give up. He took the ball to Wham-O. Wham-O was a nearby toy company. It had big success with other toys. Examples are the Frisbee® and Hula-Hoop®.

Wham-O was interested. It wanted Stingley to make the ball stronger. Stingley did tests. He came up with a perfect formula. Wham-O bought it. It dyed the ball. It sold it for just 98 cents.

Kids loved it. They bounced the ball everywhere. They bounced it to friends down the street. They bounced it against walls. They counted how many times it bounced back.

McGeorge Bundy (1919-1996)

Wham-O made about 170,000 Super Balls® daily. *Time* magazine wrote an article about its big sales. National Security Advisor McGeorge Bundy bounced one in his basement. Business executives bounced them in offices.

Many promotions followed. Wham-O made a Super Ball® the size of a bowling ball. It performed stunts. A Super Ball® was dropped from the 23rd floor of a hotel.

The hotel was in Australia. The ball bounced twice. It landed on the roof of a parked car. The car was destroyed.

The toy also inspired the name of a sporting event. The National Football League (NFL) wanted a better name for their annual football championship.

Lamar Hunt (1932-2006)

Lamar Hunt owned the Kansas City Chiefs. He got an idea. He had seen his kids playing with a Super Ball®. He proposed the game be called the Super Bowl. The media loved that idea.

Wham-O kept marketing the toy. It revived the Super Ball® in 1976 and 1998. The amazing bouncer remained popular. This is thanks to Stingley who saw something super in rubber goo.

FLOPPED!
Hasbro's 2006
Easy-Bake® Oven

Millions of kids had an Easy-Bake® Oven. This toy was launched in 1963. It was a huge hit in the 1960s. It was made by Kenner Products. By 1999, more than 16 million were sold. The Easy-Bake® Ovens really worked. They were heated by a lightbulb. They were easy to use. They were safe. Kids could bake real cakes. That changed when Hasbro took over. Hasbro is a toy company. It changed the oven's design in 2006. The original cake mix was pushed through a side slot. Hasbro modeled the new design on real ovens. It used a heating element instead of a lightbulb. The mix was loaded through a front door. The result was a disaster. Kids placed their hands inside the oven. Some were burned by the extreme heat. Five injuries were reported. The Hasbro model was removed in 2007.

LEARN MORE

Books

Merrell, Patrick. *Game On! Awesome Activities for Clever Kids: Mazes, Word Games, Hidden Pictures, Brainteasers, Spot the Differences and More!* Garden City, NY: Dover Publications, 2020.

Slater, Lee. *Play-doh Pioneer: Joseph McVicker*. Minneapolis: ABDO, 2016.

Yurich, Ginny. *1000 Hours Outside: Activities to Match Screen Time with Green Time*. New York: DK Publications, 2022.

Websites

With an adult, explore more online with these suggested searches.

"29 Best Outdoor Games for Kids of All Ages," SplashLearn

"History of Toys," TheSchoolRun

"History of Toys and Games," Mocomi Kids

GLOSSARY

chemist (KEH-mist) a scientist who studies chemicals and their properties

compound (KAHM-pownd) a substance made of 2 or more different combined chemical elements

engineer (en-juh-NEER) a designer and builder of engines or other complex structures

flop (FLAHP) to fail

jingle (JIN-guhl) a short slogan, verse, or tune designed to be easily remembered and used to promote something

manufactured (man-yuh-FAK-cherd) made in large quantities using machines

persistence (per-SIH-stuhns) the will to keep trying after first failing or experiencing challenges

pliable (PLYE-uh-buhl) easily bent or flexible

putty (PUH-tee) a doughlike soft substance used like clay

synthetic (sin-THEH-tik) something produced with chemicals instead of natural ingredients

vinyl (VYE-nuhl) strong, shiny, flexible plastic used for making things including flooring and furniture

INDEX

ABOUT THE AUTHOR

Martin Gitlin is an educational book author based in Connecticut. He won more than 45 awards as a newspaper sportswriter from 1991 to 2002. Included was a first-place award from the Associated Press for his coverage of the 1995 World Series. He has had more than 200 books published since 2006. Most of them were written for students.